GRADED
ENGLISH GRAMMAR

(INTERNATIONAL EDITION)
(with clear-cut Explanations of Grammatical Rules)

Book - 2

By
T. RAAJ BHANOT

Published by
DREAMLAND PUBLICATIONS
J-128, Kirti Nagar, New Delhi - 110 015 (India)
Tel.: 011-2510 6050, Fax : 011-2543 8283
E-mail : dreamland@vsnl.com
Shop online at www.dreamlandpublications.com
Like us on www.facebook.com/DreamlandPublications

Published in 2015 by
DREAMLAND PUBLICATIONS
J-128, Kirti Nagar, New Delhi - 110 015 (India)
Tel : 011-2510 6050, Fax : 011-2543 8283
E-mail : dreamland@vsnl.com, www.dreamlandpublications.com
Copyright © 2015 Dreamland Publications
All rights reserved. No part of this publication should be reproduced, stored in a retrieval system or transmitted in any form or by any means—electronic, mechanical, photocopying, recording or otherwise—without the prior written permission of Dreamland Publications.
ISBN 978-17-3014-086-0

Printed by : RAVE INDIA

PREFACE

Here is a series on English Grammar for the pupils of schools. It has been prepared in a uniquely graded manner and in a style that is quite off the beaten track.

The present book is meant for the pupils of class II who have just covered their elementary lessons in class I. The lessons in this volume include **A, B, C... Order,** the use of **Capital letters, base form** of the Verb, **past form** of the Verb, **shall/will** and **introductory it** and **there**.

Besides, small questions-sentences using question-words—**who, what, which, where, how, many** and **when** have also been incorporated. Necessary vocabulary and practical composition have also been included in a novel way, to kindle interest amongst students.

Illustrations have been used as the chief potent medium to teach the children basic facts of English Grammar. The author has taken pains to make the lessons quite interesting.

Another glaring feature of the series is the explanation of the rules of grammar taught in each lesson in a special box to make the teaching-learning process much easier and more effective.

With intense pleasure, I place the series in the hands of teachers of the English language and the students hoping that it will receive a befitting response. I am sure that it will serve its purpose in an admirable manner and create a place for itself over other books, flooding the market. Any suggestions for the enhancement of the book's quality shall be welcomed and duly considered for inclusion in the subsequent editions.

— **T. RAAJ BHANOT**

CONTENTS

1. A, B, C....Order 5
2. Two Sounds of U 7
3. Two Sounds of Y 9
4. Two Sounds of W 11
5. Naming Words 13
6. Me, Us, You...................... 16
7. Our, Your, Their, Its 18
8. Time 21
9. Is This...?/Is That...? 22
10. Are These...?/Are Those...?.... 25
11. What Is...?/What Are...? 28
12. The Base Form...(Positive) 31
13. The Base Form...(Negative) 32
14. The Base Form...(Questions)... 33
15. Prayer, Order, Advice (Positive) .. 34
16. Actions Going On 36
17. The Past Form...(Positive) 38
18. The Past Form...(Negative) 41
19. The Past Form...(Questions).... 43
20. Shall/Will 44
21. Short Forms 46
22. Use of Capital Letters 47
23. Describing Words 51
24. The Number 54
25. Gender 58
26. How Is It Done ?...(Manner) 61
27. When Is It Done ?...(Time) 64
28. Where Is It Done ?...(Place) 67
29. With...(For Using Instruments) ... 70
30. With...(In The Company Of) 72
31. And, But, Or 74
32. Conversation 76
33. Vocabulary 77
34. Composition 80

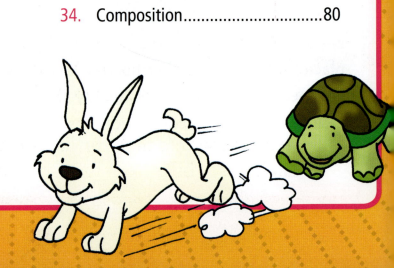

1. A, B, C.... ORDER

We know how to write *letters* in A,B,C... order. Now we shall learn how to write **words** in A, B, C... order.

A. Look at the following words and their pictures:

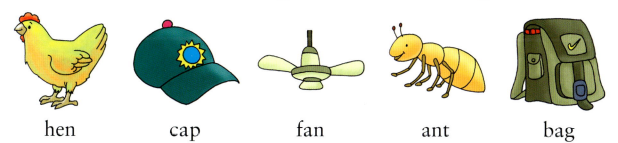

    hen   cap   fan   ant   bag

We are to write these words in A, B, C.... order.
So we shall write their first letters.
These letters are **h, c, f, a, b.**
Now we shall put these letters in A, B, C.... order.
They will be *a, b, c, f, h.*
So the above words in A, B, C.... order will be —
    ant   bag   cap   fan   hen

B. Now observe the following pictures and their words:

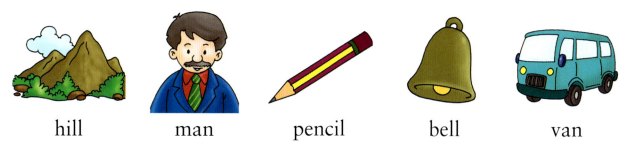

    hill   man   pencil   bell   van

The first letters of the above words are **h, m, p, b, v.**
We shall write these letters in A, B, C... order; as—
b   h   m   p   v
So the above words in A, B, C.... order will be—
    bell   hill   man   pencil   van

TEST YOURSELF

A. Write each set of letters in A, B, C.... order :

1. j   t   c   z   a   ....
2. s   b   l   p   f   ....
3. g   y   a   q   h   ....
4. n   e   w   r   b   ....
5. k   x   v   d   f   ....

B. Write each set of words in A, B, C.... order :

1. car   eat   till   say   ....
2. land   hut   ape   sun   ....
3. rod   pen   lip   dig   ....
4. mat   yes   bat   rod   ....
5. wife   girl   uncle   iron   ....

C. (a) Write five words that start with *d* :

....

(b) Now put the above words in A, B, C.... order :

....

D. (a) Write the names of *five toys* :

....

(b) Now put the above names in A, B, C.... order :

....

E. (a) Write the names of *your four class-mates* :

....

(b) Now put these names in A, B, C.... order :

....

2 TWO SOUNDS OF U

There are two different sounds of the letter **u**
One sound of **u** is an **open sound**.
The other sound of **u** is like that of **y**.

OPEN SOUND OF U:

bug   cup   drum   gun

tub   gum   jug   nut

hut   mug   pup   sun

SOUND OF U AS Y:

uniform   unity   urinal   utensils

TEST YOURSELF

A. Answer:
1. How many sounds of *u* are there? ....
2. What is one sound of *u* like? ....
3. What is the other sound of *u* like? ....

B. Speak each word. Write the sound of its *u* under it:

up	union	under	utter	unit
....	....	....	....	....
umbrella	us	umpire	unicycle	union
....	....	....	....	....

C. Look at each picture. Write the word for it. Also, write the sound of *u*:

....
....

D. Write 15 words with the open sound of *u*:

....
....
....

E. Write five words with the sound *u* as *y*:

....

3 TWO SOUNDS OF Y

The letter **y** has two different sounds.
One sound of **y** is its non-vowel sound.
The other sound of **y** is like that of **i**.

NON-VOWEL SOUND OF Y:

yak   yarn   year   you

yolk   yacht   yoke   yam

SOUND OF Y AS I:

   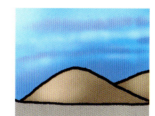

cry   dry   fly   sky

fry   ply   rye   bye-bye

TEST YOURSELF

A. Answer :

1. How many sounds of *y* are there? ....
2. What is one sound of *y* like? ....
3. What is the other sound of *y* like? ....

B. Speak each word. Write the sound of its *y* under it:

my	yell	buy	sty	guy	your
....	....	....	....	....	....
try	beyond	spy	yellow	sky	why
....	....	....	....	....	....

C. Look at each picture. Write the word for it. Also, write the sound of *y*:

....
....

D. Write 15 words with *non-vowel* sound of *y*:

....
....
....

E. Write five words with sound of *y* as *i*:

....

4 TWO SOUNDS OF W

The letter **w** has two different sounds.
One sound of **w** is like that of v.
The other sound of **w** is like that of **double u**.

SOUND OF W AS V:

| wall | watch | water | woman |

| wolf | wood | well | wheel |

SOUND OF W AS U:

| dew | ewe | mew | stew |

| howl | jowl | prowl | brown |

TEST YOURSELF

A. Answer :

1. How many sounds of *w* are there? ....
2. What is one sound of *w* like? ....
3. What is the other sound of *w* like? ....

B. Speak each word. Write the sound of its *w* under it:

new	vowel	threw	when	blew	why
....	....	....	....	....	....
word	flew	warn	crew	warm	slew
....	....	....	....	....	....

C. Look at each picture. Write the word for it. Also, write the sound of *w*:

....
....

D. Write 15 words with sound of *w* as *v*:

....
....
....

E. Write five words with sound of *w* as *u*:

....

5 NAMING WORDS

A. Look at each picture and read the sentence under it:

The **baby** is sleeping.   The **boy** and the **girl** are dancing.

The words—*baby, boy, girl*—name *persons*. They are NOUNS.

A. Look at each picture and read the sentence under it:

The girls are playing in the **park**.   We go to **school** every day.

The words—*park, school*—name **places**. They are NOUNS.

A. Look at each picture and read the sentence under it:

The **lion** is roaring aloud.   A **hare** can run very fast.

The words—*lion, hare*—name **animals**. They are NOUNS.

D. Look at each picture and read the sentence under it:

A **pen** is to write with.   We sleep on soft **beds.**

The words—*pen, beds*—name **things**. They are also NOUNS. We see that naming words are the names of *persons*, *places*, *animals* and *things*. So they all are Nouns.

TEST YOURSELF

A. Look at each picture. Write the word for it. Also, write what it names:

 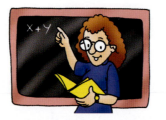 

....
....

....
....

B. Write—

(a) five nouns naming persons:
....

(b) five nouns naming animals:
....

(c) five nouns naming places:
....

(d) five nouns naming things:
....

C. Each sentence has a noun. Underline it. Also, write what it names:

1. Alfred is fair but short. ....
2. A chair is lying there. ....
3. Horses are very faithful. ....
4. We look ugly without clothes. ....
5. We worship in holy places. ....
6. The cock crows at 4-00 a.m. ....
7. Jackals are very cunning. ....
8. He lives in a small village. ....
9. A pencil is to draw with. ....

D. Write a suitable noun in each blank:

1. We cannot live without air and ....
2. John and Peter are very fast ....
3. Help the blind .... to cross the road.
4. .... and goats give us milk.
5. The baby is playing with its ....

6 ME, US, YOU

ME **YOU** **US**

Lucy is my sister. She loves **me**.

Here is your bat. I give it to **you**.

We are your friends. Do you know **us**?

He is my father. He does a lot for **me**.

Mary held a party. Did she invite **you** to it?

We were late. The teacher fined **us**.

TEST YOURSELF

A. Look at each picture and put *me*, *you* or *us* in each blank:

She is my grandma. She is telling .... a story.

Here comes daddy. He is bringing toys for ....

He is your brother. Does he help.......... in homework?

B. **Choose the right word and write it in the blank:**

1. He is a reporter. He wants to see.................. . *(your, you)*
2. Your daddy wants to speak to...................... . *(my, me)*
3. The policeman is looking at .... (our, us)
4. The bear is coming towards .... (your, you)
5. Our mother cooks food for .... (us, our)
6. The dog was chasing .... (mine, me)
7. They will give.................. sweets and marbles. (our, us)
8. I shall help ....in every way. (you, your)
9. Our friends are calling .... for play. (me, us)
10. My mummy will help.... to do my homework. (my, me)

C. **Fill up each blank with a suitable word under each picture:**

John is a good......................
He met...........yesterday in the market.

John has sent a pen for ...., Alfred.

John also gave ....a lot of sweets.

John always helps .... both. He is a very good boy.

I want to tell ....a nice joke, Alfred.

What is it? Let .... know at once.

7 OUR, YOUR, THEIR, ITS

OUR

I am Peter. You are Nancy.
We are brother and sister.
That woman is Mrs John.
She is **our** mummy.

I am Nancy. You are Peter.
We are sister and brother.
That man is Mr John.
He is **our** daddy.

YOUR, THEIR

You are Mary. He is Clark.
These are toys.
These are **your** toys.

He is Bob. She is Massy.
That is a house.
That is **their** house.

ITS

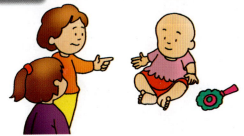

Here is a baby.
That is a rattle.
That is **its** rattle.

Here is a doll.
This is a cap.
This is **its** cap.

TEST YOURSELF

A. Look at each picture and fill up the blanks under it:

Who is this boy?
....

Who is that girl?
....

What is Peter to Nancy?
....

What is Nancy to Peter?
....

Who is this man?
....

Who is that lady?
....

What is she to him?
....

What is he to her?
....

Who are you?
....

Who is that lady?
....

What are you to her?
....

What is she to you?
....

Who are you?
....

Who is that man?
....

What are you to him?
....

What is he to you?
....

TEST YOURSELF

B. Look at each picture and fill up the blanks:

Who are you?
....
Who is she?
....
What are you to her?
....
Who is that man?
....
What is he to you both?
....

Who are you?
....
Who is he?
....
What are you to him?
....
Who is that woman?
....
What is she to you both?
....

1. Who are Peter and Nancy? ....
2. Who are Mr and Mrs John? ....
3. What is Peter to them? ....
4. What are they to Peter? ....
5. What are they to Nancy? ....

8 TIME

We often talk of time. There are six common points regarding time as under:

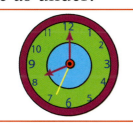
8 o'clock
8-00 a.m./p.m.

half past 8
8-30 a.m./p.m.

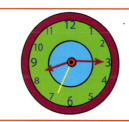
a quarter past 8
8-15 a.m./p.m.

a quarter to 8

10 minutes past 8

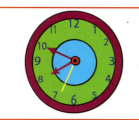
10 minutes to 8

TEST YOURSELF

Read each clock and write the time that it shows:

.... 7:00 ....

.... 7:30 ....

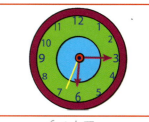
.... 6:15 ....

.... 9:45 ....

....

....

9 IS THIS…?/IS THAT…?

Is this a hen?
Yes. it is a hen.

Is that a kite?
Yes, that is a kite.

It this a cup?
Yes, it is a cup.

Is this a ball?
No, it is not a ball.
It is a bat.

Is that a jug?
No, that is not a jug.
That is a pen.

Is this a hen?
No, it is not a hen.
It is a duck.

Is this a goat or a sheep?
This is a sheep, not a goat.

Is that a cat or a dog?
That is a dog, not a cat.

Is that a chair or a table?
That is a table, not a chair.

22

TEST YOURSELF

A. Look at each picture and answer:

B. Fill up each blank:

1. Is this a dog?
   yes, ...

2. Is this a duck?
   yes, ...

3. Is that a cat?
   yes, ...

4. Is that a ball?
   yes, ...

5. Is this a crow?
   No, ...

6. Is that a goat?
   No, ...

7. Is this a chair?
   No, ...

8. Is that a pencil?
   No, ...

10 ARE THESE...?/ARE THOSE...?

Are these goats?
Yes, these are goats.

Are those dolls?
Yes, those are dolls.

Are these dogs?
Yes, these are dogs.

Are those cups?
Yes, those are cups.

Are these pencils?
No, these are pens.

Are those parrots?
No, those are crows.

Are those asses?
No, those are horses.

Are these foxes?
No, these are hares.

TEST YOURSELF

A. Look at each picture and fill up the blanks under it:

Are these apples? Are those birds?
Yes, ... Yes, ...

Are those sharpeners? Are these inkpots?
Yes, ... Yes, ...

Are these ducks? Are those chairs?
No, ... No, ...

Are those ice creams? Are these spoons?
No, ... No, ...

A. Look at each picture and answer:

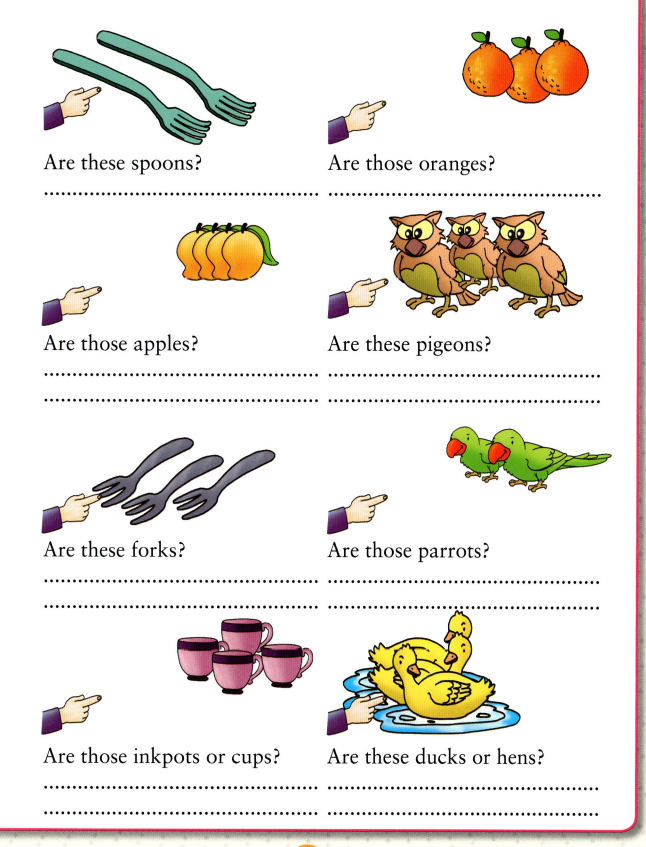

Are these spoons?

Are those oranges?

Are those apples?

Are these pigeons?

Are these forks?

Are those parrots?

Are those inkpots or cups?

Are these ducks or hens?

11 WHAT IS...?/WHAT ARE...?

What is this?
This is a cage.

What is that?
That is a hen.

What is this?
This is a bed.

What are these?
These are goats.

What are those?
Those are eggs.

What are these?
These are books.

What is this?
This is a lock.

What is that?
That is a sock.

What are these?
These are keys.

What are those?
Those are pens.

What is that?
That is a duck.

What is this?
This is an elephant.

TEST YOURSELF

A. Look at the picture and answer:

What is this? What is that? What is this?
This is .... That is .... This is ....

What are these? What are those? What is this?
These are .... Those are .... This is ....

What is that? What is this? What are these?
That is .... This is .... These are ....

What are those? What is this? What is that?
Those are .... This is .... That is ....

29

B. Look at the picture and answer:

What is this?
....

What is that?
....

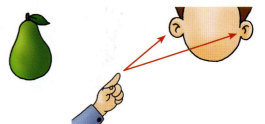
What are those?
....

What is that?
....

What is this?
....

What are these?
....

What are these?
....

What is this?
....

What are those?
....

What is that?
....

What is this?
....

What are these?
....

12 THE BASE FORM... (Positive)

Explanation of Rules:

We read about action words in Book 1.
They are used to show *actions*.
Some actions are done *now*—in the *present time*.
For these actions, we use the **base forms** of *action words*.
The base form is also called the **first form**.
We use the **base form + s/es** with *he, she, it*.

Examples:

I **go** to school daily.	**But**	He **goes** to school daily.
You **go** to school daily.		She **goes** to school daily.
We **go** to school daily.		It **goes** to school daily.
They **go** to school daily.		The boy **goes** to school daily.

TEST YOURSELF

A. Use the *correct base form* of the given action word:

1. God .... *helps* .... us in every way. *(help)*
2. I always .... *do* .... my duty well. *(do)*
3. He always .... *does* .... the right thing. *(do)*
4. She .... *has* .... full faith in God. *(have)*
5. He .... *prays* .... to God every morning. *(pray)*
6. The girl .... *sings* .... a sweet song. *(sing)*
7. Eddie always .... *speaks* .... the truth. *(speak)*
8. They .... *try* .... to be true and good. *(try)*
9. Good children .... *shun* .... bad habits. *(shun)*
10. Here is a baby. It .... *cries* .... when it is hungry. *(cry)*

13 THE BASE FORM... (Negative)

Explanation of Rules:
The base forms of action words are used for present actions. For negative present actions, we add **do not/does not** before the base form.

Examples:

Positive	Negative
I *live* in a hut.	I **do not** *live* in a hut.
We *play* under the tree.	We **do not** *play* under the tree.
You *pray* to God daily.	You **do not** *pray* to God daily.
They do their homework.	They **do not** do their homework.

But—

He *lives* in a hut.	He **does not** *live* in a hut.
She *plays* under the tree.	She **does not** *play* under the tree.
The baby cries for milk.	The baby **does not** *cry* for milk.

TEST YOURSELF

A. Change each sentence into its *negative form*:

1. The baby-bird looks up.
   ....

2. Susan sees the baby-bird.
   ....

3. I eat bread and butter in the morning.
   ....

4. We help them in every way.
   ....

5. They feel very happy here.
   ....

14 THE BASE FORM... (Questions)

Explanation of Rules:
We use **the base form** for present actions.
To make questions, we put **Do** or **Does** in the beginning.
We put a **question-mark** after every question.

Examples:

Positive	Questions
1. I tip-toe into the room.	**Do** I *tip-toe* into the room?
2. We trust in God.	**Do** *we trust in* God?
3. He does his duty well.	**Does** he do his duty well?
4. She has faith in God.	**Does** she have faith in God?
5. You do your duty well.	**Do** you do your duty well?

TEST YOURSELF

A. Change each sentence into a *question*:

1. Alex plays near the hut.
   ....

2. The baby-birds say, "tweet, tweet."
   ....

3. He always keeps his promise.
   ....

4. Alex's mother sees the baby-bird.
   ....

5. You always obey your elders.
   ....

6. We bring bread for the baby-bird.
   ....

7. The baby-bird falls down.
   ....

15 PRAYER, ORDER, ADVICE (Positive)

A. PRAYERS/REQUESTS

1. **Help** us, O Father of all.
2. **Give** me something to eat, sir.
3. **Have** pity on me, Your Majesty.
4. **Get** me a cup of tea, please.

B. ORDERS

1. **Shut** the window, Tina.
2. **Bring** me a glass of water, Todd.
3. **Open** the book on page 10.
4. **Dust** the chair at once.

C. ADVICE

1. **Be** kind to animals and birds.
2. **Get** up early in the morning.
3. **Wash** your hands before every meal.
4. **Wish** your teachers in the morning.

Explanation of Rules:
1. We use **action words** to *pray/request* for something.
2. We use action words to give *orders*.
3. We use action words to give an *advice*.
4. We use *each action word* in its **base form** to start the sentence.

TEST YOURSELF

A. Read each sentence carefully. Write whether it is a *prayer, order* **or** *advice*:

1. Always do your duty well. ....
2. Help us, O God. We are your children. ....
3. Bring me a glass of water, Clark. ....
4. Have full faith in God. ....
5. Always stick to your promise. ....
6. Get me something to drink, sir. ....
7. Do this work just now. ....
8. Always keep clean and tidy. ....
9. Bless me, O God, with your gifts. ....
10. Be off from here at once. ....

B. (a) Write two *requests* in the blanks given below:
1. ....
2. ....

(b) Write two sentences showing advice:
1. ....
2. ....

(c) Write two orders in the blanks given below:
1. ....
2. ....

16 ACTIONS GOING ON

Explanation of Rules:
An action that is going on now is in the real present action. For such actions, we use **am/is/are + base form + ing**; as :

1. I **am** working. But 5. We **are** working.
2. He **is** working. 6. You **are** working.
3. She **is** working. 7. You all **are** working.
4. It **is** working. 8. They **are** working.

TEST YOURSELF

A. Put the *real present action form* in each blank:

1. The mahout .... the elephant to the river. **(take)**
2. The herd .... before the tailor's door. **(pass)**
3. The kind tailor .... in his shop. **(sit)**
4. The tailor .... a sweet banana. **(eat)**
5. the tailor .... a banana to the elephant. **(give)**
6. The tailor .... the elephant's trunk. **(prick)**
7. The elephants .... in the river. **(bathe)**
8. The tailor .... sad and ashamed. **(feel)**
9. I .... a letter to my friend. **(write)**
10. You .... your new clothes. **(spoil)**
11. We .... our homework carefully. **(do)**
12. She .... a new shir for Erika. **(sew)**

B. Put the correct word in each blank:

1. .... am reading a very fine story.
2. .... are doing your homework neatly.

3. ……………….. is washing her dirty clothes.
4. ……………are playing with our bats and balls.
5. ……………….. are cleaning their class-room.
6. ………………is dressing his hair with a comb.
7. Here is a baby. ……………….. is crying for milk.

C. **Make the *ing-forms*. One is done for you:**

1. take   ...taking.....
2. read   ………………
3. talk   ………………
4. run   ………………
5. sleep ………………
6. jump   ………………
7. live   ………………
8. get   ………………
9. fill   ………………
10. shoot ………………
11. drink ………………
12. stop ………………

D. **Look at each picture and write a sentence for it in *real present action form*:**

……………………………………………………   ……………………………………………………

……………………………………………………   ……………………………………………………

17. THE PAST FORM... (Positive)

Explanation of Rules:
1. An action may be done *now* or in *the past*.
2. We use **base form** of the *action word* for the *present action*
3. We use its **past form** for the *past action*.

Examples:

A. PRESENT ACTIONS   PAST ACTIONS

1. Tina **is** a small girl.   Tina **was** a small girl.
2. Tina **is** slim and fair.   Tina **was** slim and fair
3. The tree **has** many leaves.   The tree **had** many leaves.
4. The baby-birds **are** hungry.   The baby-birds **were** hungry.

LEARN THE FOLLOWING:

Base Form	Past Form	Base Form	Past Form
is, am	was	call	called
are	were	look	looked
have, has	had	fall	fell
help	helped	see	saw
do	did	take	took
run	ran	shout	shouted
come	came	get	got
live	lived	bring	brought
play	played	say	said
eat	ate	reply	replied

B. You learnt to use **there is/there are** in your class I as under:

(a) There **is** a baby-bird in the nest.
(b) There **are** two baby-birds in the nest.

In the past form, they will be—

(a) there **was** a baby-bird in the nest.
(b) There **were** two baby-birds in the nest.

TEST YOURSELF

A. Write the past forms of:

Base Form	Past Form	Base Form	Past Form
has, have	....	thank	....
are	....	say	....
hop	....	am	....
help	....	eat	....
bring	....	run	....
call	....	put	....

B. Change each sentence into its past form:

1. Kate puts the bird on the grass.
   ....

2. The mother-bird is away from the nest.
   ....

3. The baby-birds are hungry.
   ....

4. Kate takes the baby-bird to her mother.
   ....

5. The baby-birds thank Kate.
   ....

6. The baby-bird eats bread.
   ....

7. There is a man in the room.
   ....

8. There are four men in the room.
   ....

9. Cars run up and down the road.

   ....

10. The mother calls out her children.

    ....

C. *(a)* Write four sentences starting with *there was*:

1. ....
2. ....
3. ....
4. ....

(b) Write four sentences starting with there *were*:

1. ....
2. ....
3. ....
4. ....

(D) Look at each picture and write a sentence for it in *past action form*:

....

....

18 THE PAST FORM... (Negative)

Explanation of Rules:
To make the negative of the past form, we—
(a) use **did not** before the action word.
(b) change its *past form* into **base form**.

Examples:

Oppsitive
1. A cat **lived** in an old house.
2. Many rats also **lived** in that house.
3. The rats **danced** in joy.

Nagetive:
1. A cat **did not** live in an old house.
2. Many rats **did not** live in that house.
3. The rats **did not** dance in joy.

TEST YOURSELF

A. Change the *action word* into its *past form*:

1. Many rats live in an old house.
   ....
2. A cat also lives in that house.
   ....
3. The cat calls the rats to her.
   ....
4. All the rats play together.
   ....
5. The rats come out of their holes.
   ....

6. The rats bow before the cat.
   ....

7. The rats like the cat very much.
   ....

8. The rats walk up to the cat in turn.
   ....

9. The cat waits for the rats.
   ....

10. The cat runs out of the old house.
    ....

B. Give the past form:

Base Form	Past Form	Base Form	Past Form
live	....	run	....
make	....	sit	....
like	....	call	....
bow	....	come	....
tell	....	like	....
dig	....	eat	....

C. Change each sentence into its *negative* form:

1. The rats dug holes to live in.
   ....

2. The rats liked the cat.
   ....

3. The rats bowed before the cat.
   ....

4. Kitty came last of all.
   ....

19 THE PAST FORM... (Questions)

Explanation of Rules:
To make questions with the past form of action words, we—
(a) use **Did** in the *beginning* of the sentence.
(b) change the *past form* to the **base form**.

Examples:

Positive	Questions
1. Kim **lost** her dog.	**Did** Kim *lose* her dog ?
2. Todd **looked** for the dog.	**Did** Todd *look* for the dog ?
3. The dog **slept** in peace.	**Did** the dog *sleep* in peace ?
4. Todd **felt** very chilly.	**Did** Todd *feel* very chilly ?

TEST YOURSELF

Change each sentence into a question:

1. The gardener hurled a shoe at Todd.
   ....

2. The landlord threw water on Todd.
   ....

3. The dog barked loudly at me.
   ....

4. I went home quickly.
   ....

5. You helped me in every way.
   ....

6. We bought apples and oranges.
   ....

7. She fixed a rose in her hair.
   ....

20 SHALL/WILL

Explanation of Rules:
Some actions are not done in the *time going on*. They are to be done in the **time to come**. For them, we use **shall/will** before the **base forms of action words**. We use **shall** with *I, we*. But we use **will** with *he, she, it, you* and *they*.

Examples:

I **shall** *work*.
We **shall** *work*.
You **will** *work*.
You all **will** *work*.
The boy **will** *work*.

He **will** *work*.
She **will** *work*.
It **will** *work*.
They **will** *work*.
The boys **will** *work*.

TEST YOURSELF

A. Write *will* or *shall* in each blank :

1. Ashley .... celebrate her birthday on 10th August.
2. She .... hold a tea-party on her birthday.
3. She .... invite her friends to this party.
4. I .... also go to attend this party.
5. Jack and Jill .... make a pillow-hill.
6. They .... climb up the pillow-hill.
7. We .... reap the crop in summer.
8. The ant .... work all day to collect food.
9. I .... succeed or die in the attempt.
10. I think we .... win the match.
11. He .... do as I bid him.
12. You .... obey my orders.

B. Here is a talk between an ant and a cricket. Fill up each blank with the correct word :

1. **Cricket** : Hello Miss Ant ! how are .... ?
2. **Ant** : Fine, thank you. How are you ? What .... you here ?
3. **Cricket** : I.............. nothing to eat. Give me some food.
4. **Ant** : Didn't you .... any food in summer ?
5. **Cricket** : No, Miss. I did not store any .... then.
6. **Ant** : What were you .... then ?
7. **Cricket** : I was .... the whole day long.
8. **Ant** : You must .... all day now. Go away. I have .... food for you.
9. The cricket went away .... and ashamed.

C. Read the example. Then fill up each blank with the correct form of the action word:

1. We..............sleep.................... indoors in winter. *(sleep)*
2. I .... to do things in time. *(learn)*
3. The labourer .... hard all day. *(work)*
4. They..................................... at the poor beggar. *(laugh)*
5. Jill .... down the pillow-hill. *(roll)*
6. Jack...flat on the floor. *(fall)*
7. The farmers................... the wheat-crop in April. *(reap)*
8. You all ....to Ashley's party on Sunday. *(go)*
9. The cricket .... of hunger in winter. *(die)*
10. Mother........................... sweet pudding for us. *(cook)*
11. She .... us a very sweet song. *(sing)*

21 SHORT FORMS

We write some words in short forms as under:

Full Form	Short form	Full Form	Short Form
I am	**I'm**	do not	**don't**
I shall	**I'll**	does not	**doesn't**
I had	**I'd**	did not	**didn't**
I have	**I've**	he will	**he'll**
Will not	**won't**	are not	**aren't**
Was not	**wasn't**	were not	**weren't**
Is not	**isn't**	cannot	**can't**

TEST YOURSELF

Write the words in italics in their short forms:

1. *I shall* help you in every way.
   ....
2. *Do not* spit on the clean floor.
   ....
3. *I am* feeling very uneasy.
   ....
4. This book is *not* mine.
   ....
5. I *cannot* give you this book.
   ....
6. He *was not* a good artist.
   ....
7. She *will not* let you enter her house.
   ....

22 USE OF CAPITAL LETTERS

Explanation of Rules:
English was written using only capital letters in the past. But then the writers developed small letters. So capital letters are used today as under :

1. The *first letter* of the *first word* of a sentence; as—
   - (a) The boys are playing in the park.
   - (b) Honesty is the best policy.

2. The *first letter* of the *first word* of each line of a poem; as—

   Boys and girls !
   Come out to play ;
   This is the only way,
   To be happy and gay.

3. The *first letters* of names of *days, months, festivals*; as—
   - (a) We shall come to see you on **Tuesday**.
   - (b) The **Christmas** falls in the month of **December**.

4. The *first letters* of the *proper names* of people and places; as—
   - (a) **Alexander** was a brave general.
   - (b) **London** is the capital the U.K.

5. The *first letters* of the names of *rivers, mountains, buildings* ; as—
   - (a) The river **Thames** flows through London.
   - (b) The **Himalayas** are the highest mountains.
   - (c) The **Taj Mahal** is in India.

6. The *first letters* of the names of *school subjects* ; as—
   (a) **English** is spoken in all the countries.
   (b) **Mathematics** is a tough subject.

7. The *letters* of the *abbreviations* are mostly *capital*; as—
   (a) Prime Minister **PM**   (c) Please Turn Over   **PTO**
   (b) Station Master **SM**   (d) General Post-Office **GPO**

8. The *first letters* of the names of *seas* and *oceans*; as—
   Red Sea   Black Sea   Pacific Ocean

9. Letters *I, O* when used alone as words; as—
   (a) **I** am a student of class II.
   (b) Help me, **O** God, out of this trouble.

TEST YOURSELF

A. Here is a list of 15 words. Six of them must begin with capital letters. Sort them out and write them in the blanks:

orange	julie	tuesday	well	desk
zebra	alps	soil	english	table
england	sister	teacher	plate	christmas

....

B. Fill in the following table:

Your Name ....

Your Father's Name ....

Your Town/Village ....

Your School ....

C. Write the—

    (a) names of your *state* and its *two important towns*:

    ....

    (b) names of the *latest film* you have seen, its *hero* and *heroine*:

    ....

    (c) two *subjects* in which you are weak:

    ....

    (d) two *hill-stations* that you have visited:

    ....

D. Rewrite each sentence using capital letters where needed:

1. mind your own business.

   ....

2. all is not gold that glitters.

   ....

3. how sweet this rose smells!

   ....

4. how foolish I have been!

   ....

5. work while you work, ... ,
   and play while you play ;   .... ;
   this is the best way, ... ,
   to be happy and gay.   .... ;

6. the p.m. will appear on tv today.

   ....

7. the eid is a religious festival.
    ....

8. The arabian sea is to the west of india.
    ....

9. english is a common language.
    ....

10. the bible is a holy book of the christians.
    ....

11. george will tell us a story.
    ....

12. julie was john's faithful wife.
    ....

13. mr smith is our principal.
    ....

14. susan is a very intelligent girl.
    ....

E. Write the abbreviations for:

1. Money Order   ....
2. Post-Office   ....
3. Sub-Inspector   ....
4. Special Police officer ....
5. Station House officer ....
6. Railway Mail Service   ....
7. Master of Arts   ....
8. Finance Minister   ....

23 DESCRIBING WORDS

Explanation of Rules:
We use describing words before **nouns** to show their qualities.

a **red** rose

a **blue** frock

green grass

hot tea

a **cold** drink

a **round** table

Examples:
1. The word—**red**—describes the noun *rose*.
2. The word—**blue**—describes the noun *frock*.
3. The word—**green**—describes the noun *grass*.
4. The word—**hot**—describes the noun *tea*.
5. The word—**cold**—describes the noun *drink*.
6. The word—**round**—describes the noun *table*.

All the words in bold type are **describing words**.

TEST YOURSELF

A. Look at each picture. Write a proper describing word in the blank below it:

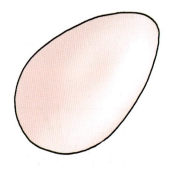  

a .... egg   a .... hen   a .... leaf

a .... man   the .... sky.   the .... sun

 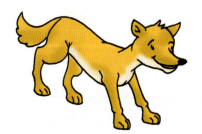 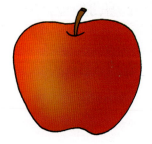

a .... crow   a .... fox   a .... apple

B. Write a noun in each blank:

1. a slim ....   2. a dirty ....   3. curly ....
4. a narrow ....   5. a naughty ....   6. an old ....
7. a deep ....   8. a sharp ....   9. green ....
10. a ripe ....   11. a dark ....   12. a lovely ....

C. Write a suitable *describing word* in each blank:

1. a .... shirt   2. a .... frock   3. an .... man
4. a .... girl   5. a .... night   6. an .... sum
7. a .... child   8. a .... skirt   9. a .... mango

D. Write each *describing word* in its own blank:

| sweet | big | heavy | beautiful | juicy |
| cunning | warm | narrow | faithful | cold |

1. Mangoes are .... and ....
2. The dog is a ....animal.
3. Germany is not a ....country.
4. We have .... drinks in summer.
5. I can lift this .... stone.
6. Susan is a .... actress.
7. This is a very ....lane.
8. Once there was a .... jackal.
9. We wear .... clothes in winter.

E. Match each *describing word* with its *noun* :

Describing Words   *Nouns*

poor   sunlight

rich   night

brave   medicine

sweet   merchant

bitter   beggar

dark   soldier

bright   mango

24 THE NUMBER

Explanation of Rules:
Nouns name *people*, *places*, *animals* and *things*.
There are nouns that can be *counted*. They are called **countable nouns**; as : *boy, cat, top* etc.

There are nouns that *cannot be counted*. They are called **uncountable nouns**; as : *milk, wheat, honey* etc.

Examples:

countable   uncountable

COUNTABLE NOUNS

A countable noun may stand for **one thing** *only*.
It may name **more-than-one** things.
Here are some examples :

cup	only one	**cups**	many
yak	only one	**yaks**	many
man	only one	**men**	many
bush	only one	**bushes**	many

SINGULARS AND PLURALS

A countable noun naming *one thing* is of **singular number**.
A countable noun naming *many things* is of **plural number**.

LEARN THE FOLLOWING :

A

Singular	Plural	Singular	Plural
ant	ants	inn	inns
ball	balls	jar	jars
bell	bells	kite	kites
boy	boys	lamp	lamps
car	cars	mat	mats
cat	cats	mouth	mouths
day	days	owl	owls
desk	desks	pot	pots
egg	eggs	star	stars
fan	fans	top	tops
girl	girls	vest	vests
goat	goats	wall	walls
hat	hats	year	years
hen	hens	zebra	zebras

B

child	children	mouse	mice
foot	feet	ox	oxen
goose	geese	tooth	teeth
man	men	woman	women

C

deer	deer	sheep	sheep
fish	fish	fruit	fruit

D

Singular	Plural	Singular	Plural
I	we	you	you
he/she/it	they	my	our
me	us	this	these
him/her	them	that	those

TEST YOURSELF

A. Write the plurals :

1. sheep ....
2. cat ....
3. man ....
4. mango ....
5. tooth ....
6. mouse ....
7. ox ....
8. fish ....
9. goose ....
10. boy ....
11. cow ....
12. orange ....
13. foot ....
14. child ....
15. girl ....
16. grape ....
17. deer ....
18. teacher ....
19. woman ....
20. man ....

B. Write the singulars :

1. .... vests
2. .... boys
3. .... these
4. .... teeth
5. .... dogs
6. .... children
7. .... sheep
8. .... keys
9. .... owls
10. .... hens
11. .... ants
12. .... feet

13. .... oxen   14. .... geese
15. ....bananas   16. .... men
17. ....women   18. .... desks

C. Change the number :

1. geese ....   2. her   ....
3. our   ....   4. it   ....
5. day   ....   6. sheep ....
7. fish   ....   8. tooth ....
9. lice   .... 10. vests ....
11. goose .... 12. man   ....

D. Rewrite each sentence changing the number of its nouns :

1. This is my book.   ....
2. A child is fussy.   ....
3. Our teeth are white.   ....
4. Children are careless.   ....
5. A cat kills a mouse.   ....
6. That is an egg.   ....
7. This is my book.   ....
8. I am a boy.   ....
9. They are players.   ....
10. These tables are round.   ....
11. Those women are nurses.   ....
12. Here are many apples.   ....
13. There are many cows.   ....
14. You all are good boys.   ....

25 THE GENDER

Explanation of Rules:
Nouns name *people* and *animals*.
A *person* may be a **male** or a **female**.
An *animal* may also be a **male** or a **female**.
A male person or animal is of **masculine gender.**
A female person or animal is of **feminine gender.**

Examples:

MALES

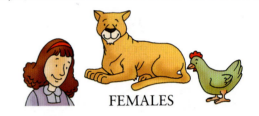
FEMALES

LEARN THE FOLLOWING :

A

Masculine	Feminine	Masculine	Feminine
boy	girl	lion	lioness
lad	lass	hunter	huntress
man	woman	tiger	tigress
prince	princess	bridegroom	bride
king	queen	father	mother
master	mistress	son	daughter
uncle	aunt	emperor	empress
bull	cow	fox	vixen
monk	nun	nephew	niece

B

he	she	his	her
he-goat	she-goat	milkman	milkmaid
cock-sparrow	hen-sparrow	peacock	peahen
tom-cat	she-cat	bull-elephant	cow-elephant

58

TEST YOURSELF

A. Write—

(a) five nouns naming masculine persons:

....

(b) five nouns naming feminine persons:

....

(d) five nouns naming masculine animals:

....

(e) five nouns naming feminine animals:

....

B. Write the *feminines*:

1. uncle ....
2. lion ....
3. nephew ....
4. monk ....
5. peacock ....
6. prince ....
7. lad ....
8. boy ....
9. nephew ....
10. master ....
11. bull ....
12. son ....
13. he-goat ....
14. fox ....

C. Write the *masculines*:

1. wife ....
2. daughter ....
3. queen ....
4. bride ....
5. aunt ....
6. niece ....
7. nun ....
8. vixen ....
9. she-goat ....
10. milkmaid ....
11. cow ....
12. lioness ....

D. Change the *gender* :

1. lion .... 2. goose ....
3. vixen .... 4. empress ....
5. bride .... 6. prince ....
7. uncle .... 8. woman ....
9. cow .... 10. madam ....

E. Rewrite each sentence *changing the gender* of each noun :

1. The king paid a visit to his mother.
   ....

2. May he come in, madam ?
   ....

3. Monks are men of great purity.
   ....

4. The milkman met a tigress on the way.
   ....

5. Girls can't be men and bulls can't be cows.
   ....

6. The bride is a very charming lass.
   ....

7. Her uncle sent her a costly present.
   ....

8. The tigress sprang at the cow and killed it.
   ....

9. My nephew sent me a message.
   ....

26 HOW IS IT DONE?... (Manner)

Explanation of Rules:
The words that **show** the manner of the actions of *verbs* are called **adverbs of manner.**

Examples:

A hare *runs* **fast**

A tortoise *moves* **slowly.**

A lion *roars* **loudly.**

You do your *hair* **carefully.**

I can *break* it **easily.**

The soldiers *fight* **bravely.**

The words—*fast, slowly, loudly, carefully, easily, bravely*—show **how** actions are done. In other words, they show the **manner** in which actions are done.

So these words are called ADVERBS OF MANNER.

TEST YOURSELF

D. Choose the right word and write it in the blank:

The lady shouted ...."Fire! fire !!"
(loudly, softly)

Girls are dancing ....
(sadly, happily)

She is reading a book ....
(silently, noisily)

The father patted his son ....
(lovingly, angrily)

The teacher slapped the student..........
(kindly, angrily)

The mother kissed the baby.................
(hatefully, lovingly)

Peter writes English quite ....
(dirtily, neatly)

B. Fill up each blank with a suitable word from the list to complete the story:

suddenly   soundly   angrily   playfully
humbly   quickly   kindly   wildly

A lion was sleeping .... under a tree.

A mouse came there ....

The mouse jumped over the lion's body ....

The lion woke up ....

The lion caught the mouse .... in his paw.

The mouse prayed for mercy ....

The lion laughed .... at its prayer.

Then the lion let the mouse off ....

27 WHEN IS IT DONE?... (Time)

Explanation of Rules:
The words that tell the time of the actions shown by verbs are called **adverbs of time.**

Examples:

I get up **early.**

He *reached* school **late.**

She *bought* a new frock **yesterday**

We shall *go* boating **today.**

It *will* be sunday **tomorrow.**

Are you doing your home work **now?**

The words—*early, late, yesterday, today, tomorrow, now,*—show **when** actions are done. So they are ADVERBS OF TIME.

TEST YOURSELF

A. Choose the right word and write it in the blank:

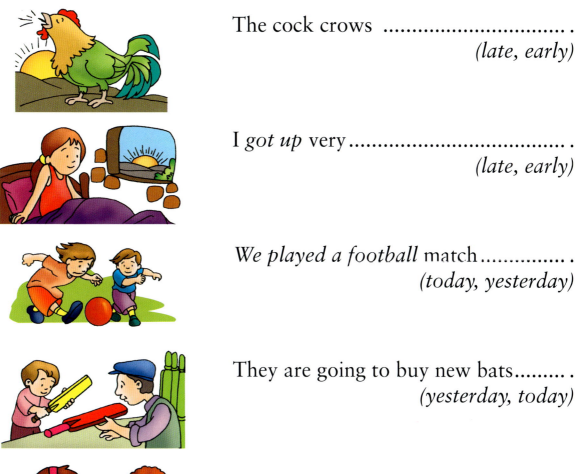

The cock crows ....
(late, early)

I *got up* very ....
(late, early)

We *played a football* match ....
(today, yesterday)

They are going to buy new bats ....
(yesterday, today)

Will you come to see me .... ?
(yesterday, tomorrow)

What time is it .... ?
(now, then)

Were you in the park .... ?
(now, then)

B. Fill up each blank with a suitable word from the list to complete the story:

immediately   early   today   late
then   yesterday   now   tomorrow

John got up very.................... today.

He put on his clothes............. and went to the park.

He met a friend on the way. So he reached the park.........

He was sorry not to find the fairy in the park ....

The fairy had promised .... to meet him in the park.

John said to himself, "What should I do ....?"

Feeling sad, John came back to his house ....

John said to himself, "I must try my luck ...."

28 WHERE IS IT DONE?... (Place)

Explanation of Rules:
The words that **show** the places of the actions of *verbs* are called **adverbs of place.**

Examples:

It is very hot **here**.

What are you doing **there**?

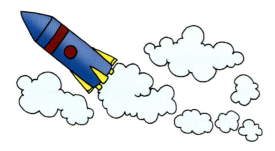

The rocket went **up** at once.

The cat is sitting there **below**.

Dry leaves are falling **down**.

Look at the sky **above**.

The words—*here, there, up, below, down, above*—show **where** actions are done. In other words, they show the **places** at which actions are done. So they are ADVERBS OF PLACE.

TEST YOURSELF

A. Choose the right word and write it in the blank:

It is very cold ....
(down, here)

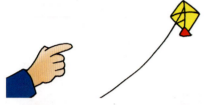

Look at that kite flying ....
(below, above)

James! What are you doing ....?
(there, up)

Vapour is lighter than air. So, it rises
.... (down, up)

The stone sank ....into the water.
(under, down)

Look ....; how clear the water
of the lake is! (below, above)

March .... and fire at the enemy.?
(ahead, front)

B. Fill up each blank with a suitable word from the list to complete the story:

| here | down | there |
| up | above | away |

The wolf growled, "What are you doing……………?"

"I am drinking water…………, sir," said the lamb.

"Why are you making water dirty……………?" said the wolf.

"No, sir. The water is coming ……. from you to me" replied the lamb.

"Come ……………, you rascal" thundered the wolf.

The lamb went …………… to the wolf trembling in fear.

Suddenly, a heavy stone rolled from …….. and it killed the wolf.

The lamb thanked God and went ………………………………

29 WITH... (For using instruments)

Explanation of Rules:
We use **with** before the instruments that we use for something.

Examples:

James is cutting the apple **with** a *knife*.

A good child alway eats **with** a *spoon*.

She is cutting a ribbon **with** *scissors*.

He killed the snake **with** a *stone*.

TEST YOURSELF

A. Put the right word in each blank:

Stella is doing her hair with a ....

John is cleaning his teeth with a ....

The wood-cutter is chopping wood with an ....

He is wiping his hands with a ....

He is writing a letter with a ....

The farmer is digging the ground with a ....

Julie is drawing a picture with a ....

The farmer is tying the bundle with a ....

The lady is washing clothes with ....

The girl is covering the cage with a ....

30 WITH... (In the company of)

Explanation of Rules:
We use **with** before the nouns that give company.

Examples:

She is going to the market **with** *her mother.*

Each of us live **with** our *parents.*

I play **with** *my friends* every day.

The hare is having a race **with** a *tortoise.*

TEST YOURSELF

A. Fill up each blank with the right word:

Mac is going to school with his ....

Peter is playing in the park with his ....

The baby is sleeping with its ………………………………… .

The duck is in the pond with its ………………………………… .

John is playing chess with his ………………………………… .

We went for a picnic with our ………………………………… .

Alfred's dog is fighting with a ………………………………… .

The father is going to the circus with his ………………………………… .

The frog wants to play with the ………………………………… .

I am playing carom with my ………………………………… .

31 AND, BUT, OR

Explanation of Rules:
The words that join sentences together are called **joning words.**

Examples:

Parents **and** *children* make a family.

She has a *son* **and** a *daughter*

Ashley is tall **but** Kim is short

Your brother is clever **but** lazy.

You can write with a *pen* **or** a *pencil*

You can go there by *bus* **or** by *train*.

and is used to join **like things**
but is used to join **opposite things**
or is used to join **things for a choice**

TEST YOURSELF

A. Choose the correct word and write it in the blank :

1. I have a toy-car ……………………… a top. *(and, but)*
2. This cloth is very fine ……………… costly. *(but, and)*
3. Which colour do you like—red …………blue ? *(and, or)*
4. An elephant is big ……………… a rat is small. *(or, but)*
5. Clark ………………….Eddie are fast friends. *(but, and)*
6. Whose bat is this—Peter's ……………Todd's ? *(but, or)*
7. The wife is tall ………… the husband is short. *(or, but)*
8. I have bread ……………… butter for breakfast. *(but, and)*
9. This basket has apples ……that one has pears. *(or, but)*
10. Days are longer ….. nights shorter in summer. *(but, and)*
11. You may stay here ………………go home now. *(but, or)*
12. You should come with your father ….mother. *(or, but)*
13. You may eat eggs ………… bread for breakfast. *(but, or)*
14. Patients and children feed on milk ……. fruit. *(or, and)*
15. I can break ………………… I cannot bend. *(and, but)*

B. Look at each picture and fill up each blank:

Q. Is this a pen……..pencil ?
A. This is not a pencil………..
   a pen.

Q. What do you wear ?
A. I wear a skirt……………..
   a blouse

32 CONVERSATION

A. Answer each question ?

1. Who are you ? ....
2. What are you ? ....
3. Who is your father ? ....
4. What is your father ? ....
5. What day is it today ? ....
6. What time is it now ? ....
7. When do you get up ? ....
8. When do you go to bed ? ....
9. How do you go to school ? ....
10. When is your school over ? ....

B Answer these questions :

1. When does your birthday fall ?
   ....
2. Which is your favourite dish ?
   ....
3. Which is your favourite subject ?
   ....
4. Who teaches you English ?
   ....
5. What colour is your hair ?
   ....
6. When does your school start ?
   ....

33 VOCABULARY

I. MONTHS OF THE YEAR

To begin with, a year had 10 months. It is clear from—

| September | 7th month | October | 8th month |
| November | 9th month | December | 10th month |

Emperor Julius Caesar of Rome added the month of **July**.
Emperor Augustus of Rome added the month of **August**.
So the year has twelve months as under :

Month	Days	Month	Days	Month	Days
January	31	February	28/29	March	31
April	30	May	31	June	30
July	31	August	31	September	30
October	31	November	30	December	31

II. CRIES OF ANIMALS

1. Asses *bray*
2. Bears *growl*
3. Bees *hum*
4. Birds *chirp*
5. Bulls *bellow*
6. Camels *grunt*
7. Cats *mew*
8. Cows *low*
9. Cocks *crow*
10. Crows *caw*
11. Dogs *bark*
12. Ducks *quack*
13. Goats *bleat*
14. Elephants *trumpet*
15. Geese *cackle*
16. Lions *roar*
17. Hens *Cluck*
18. Horses *neigh*
19. Sheep *bleat*
20. Snakes *hiss*
21. Tigers *growl*

III. YOUNG-ONES OF ANIMALS

Animal	Young-one	Animal	Young-one
ass	**foal**	goose	**gosling**
cat	**kitten**	hen	**chicken**

cow	**calf**	kangaroo	**joey**
dog	**pup**	lion	**cub**
eagle	**eaglet**	swan	**cygnet**
goat	**kid**	sheep	**lamb**
duck	**duckling**	pig	**piglet**

IV. HOMES

(a)
Person	Home	Person	Home
king	**palace**	nun	**convent**
man	**house**	prisoner	**prison**
monk	**monastery**	soldier	**barrack**

(b)
Animal	Home	Animal	Home
bird	**nest**	cow	**shed**
dog	**kennel**	rabbit	**form**
hen	**coop**	horse	**stable**
lion	**den**	mouse	**hole**
pig	**sty**	sheep	**pen**
snake	**hole**	spider	**cob-web**

V. COMMON PHRASES

1. **get up** — *to rise* : I get up at 5-00 a.m. every day.
2. **put on** — *to wear* : Put on your school uniform.
3. **put off** — *take off* : I put off (took off) my hat.
4. **give up** — *to leave* : Give up all your bad habits.
5. **leave for** — *to go to* : He left for New york yesterday.
6. **go through** — *to read* : I have gone through this book.
7. **get through** — *to pass* : She will get through the test.
8. **bring up** — *to rear* : Parents bring up their children.
9. **look after** — *care for* : Mothers look after homes.
10. **get into** — *to be in* : He has got into bad company.

VI. KNOW THE DIFFERENCE

1. **by, buy**

    The man sat *by* himself. *Buy* a new book.

2. **there, their**

    Who comes *there*? These are *their* books.

3. **son, sun**

    She has an only *son*. The *sun* sets in the west.

4. **here, hear**

    Come *here*, Shaw. I can't *hear* your voice.

5. **made, maid**

    This table is made of wood. The maid washed the cups.

6. **blew, blue**

    The watchman *blew* his whistle. Her ribbons are *blue*.

7. **red, read**

    Red apples are ripe. I have *read* this story.

8. **rode, road**

    We *rode* a horse to go there. This *road* is very wide.

9. **hair, hare**

    Her *hair* is brown. A *hare* can run very fast.

10. **weak, week**

    He is *weak* in English. Seven days make a *week*.

11. **meat, meet**

    Some people do not eat *meat*. *Meet* me in my office.

12. **be, bee**

    Always *be* in time. *Bees* collect honey for us.

34 COMPOSITION

1. THE COW

A. Fill up each blank:

1. The cow is a .... animal.
2. It has .... legs and .... horns.
3. It has a long .... also.
4. It has an .... with four teats.
5. It gives us sweet .... daily.
6. Cow's milk is very useful to small ....
7. Cow's calves grow up into cows and ....
8. Cows give us milk and oxen work for ....
9. The cow is a .... animal for the indians.
10. We call it MOTHER COW.

B. Now write these sentences as an essay:

....
....
....
....
....
....
....
....
....
....

2. OUR CLASS-ROOM

A. Fill up each blank:

1. I read in .... School.
2. Our school has classes .... to V.
3. I am in class ....
4. Our school has ....
5. Our classroom is a .... classroom.
6. It has .... desks and.................... benches.
7. These desks are lying in.. rows.
8. There is a black board on one of the............................
9. Three ....are also there.
10. Our classroom has ....door and ....windows.
11. Our classroom is very ....and well-lighted.
12. There are a table and a.................... also for the teacher.

13. There are two charts on the ....
14. Our teacher keeps his..on the task.
15. We all keep our classroom clean and................................

B. Now write these sentences in the form of an essay:

3. THE SILLY GOAT

A. Fill up each blank:

1. One day, a hungry fox was .... in a forest.
2. There was an old.................................by the way-side.
3. It was nightfall. The fox could not ....the well.
4. Suddenly it fell into the ....
5. It tried hard to .... out of the well but it could not.
6. So, it had to pass the ....in the well.
7. Next morning, a.............chanced to come near the well.
8. She peeped into the well and saw the ....in it.
9. The goat said to the fox, "Hello Mr Fox! what are you ....there in the well."
10. The fox was very.................... . It replied, "I was feeling .... So I came down to drink the cool water here. You can also come down and .... this cool water."
11. The goat was very silly. So it .... into the well at once.

12. When she had drunk water, the .... fox said to her, "If you let me .... on your shoulders. I will get out of the well. Then I shall .... you also to get out."

13. The silly goat agreed. The fox got onto her .... and came out of the well leaving the goat there.

B. Now write these sentences in the form of an essay:

....
....
....
....
....
....
....
....
....
....
....
....
....
....
....
....
....
....

4. THE GREEDY DOG

A. Fill up each blank:

1. Once there was a stray .... It was very ....
2. It was roaming in search of ....
3. Soon it came to a butcher's ....
4. The dog stole a piece of .... from the butcher's shop.
5. It ran out of the town to a..................................place.
6. It wanted to enjoy the piece of .... alone.
7. Soon it reached a stream with a ....over it.
8. The dog got onto the bridge to......................the stream.
9. Suddenly it looked at the......................... of the stream.
10. It saw its ....into the water of the stream.
11. The dog was not very .... It was very...........indeed.
12. It thought, " There is another dog with a piece of meat inside the..."

13. So it decided to snatch the……………………of that dog.
14. At once, it jumped into the ……………barking………… .
15. Its own piece of meat fell into the ………………………. .
16. Now the dog felt ashamed as well as ……………………… .
17. It went away cursing itself for its …………………………. .

B. Now write these sentences in the form of a story:

……………………………………………………………………………
……………………………………………………………………………
……………………………………………………………………………
……………………………………………………………………………
……………………………………………………………………………
……………………………………………………………………………
……………………………………………………………………………
……………………………………………………………………………
……………………………………………………………………………
……………………………………………………………………………
……………………………………………………………………………
……………………………………………………………………………
……………………………………………………………………………
……………………………………………………………………………
……………………………………………………………………………
……………………………………………………………………………
……………………………………………………………………………
……………………………………………………………………………
……………………………………………………………………………

4. APPLICATION FOR LEAVE FOR AN URGENT WORK

The Principal,
Eton school,
England,
Dated :   25th August, 2014.

Sir,

I have to visit my cousin who is down with fever. So I cannot attend school today. Kindly grant me leave for today only. I shall be very thankful to you.

Yours obediently,
Mary Johnson,
Class II-A.

TEST YOURSELF

Apply to your Principal for leave for an urgent work.

..............................,
..............................,
....
....
....

....
....
....
....

..............................,
..............................,
....

6. APPLICATION FOR LEAVE TO ATTEND A WEDDING

The principal,
Eton school,
England.
Dated : 18th March, 2014.

Sir,

The wedding of my elder sister falls tomorrow. So I cannot attend school for three days. I request you to grant me leave for three days. I shall be gradeful to you, sir.

Yours obediently,
Todd Johnson,
Class II-A.

TEST YOURSELF

Apply to your Principal for leave to attend a marriage.

……………………………,
……………………………,
………………………….
………………………….
……………….

………………………………………………………………………….
………………………………………………………………………….
………………………………………………………………………….
………………………………………………………………………….

……………………………,
……………………………,
………………………….